PELÉ

King of Football

1958 World Cup

① Brazil 2 - Sweden 1
And now Pelé takes the ball from the air . . . . . . It goes from his leg to his foot . . .
. . . He does a "bicycle". . .
No - yes. It's a goal! What a goal!
Brazil 3 - Sweden 1
Brazil are going to win this World Cup

② Who is this Pelé?

Pelé. Pelé.

③ Who is this Pelé? He is a little black boy from Brazil . . . Come with me. I'm going to take you there. . .

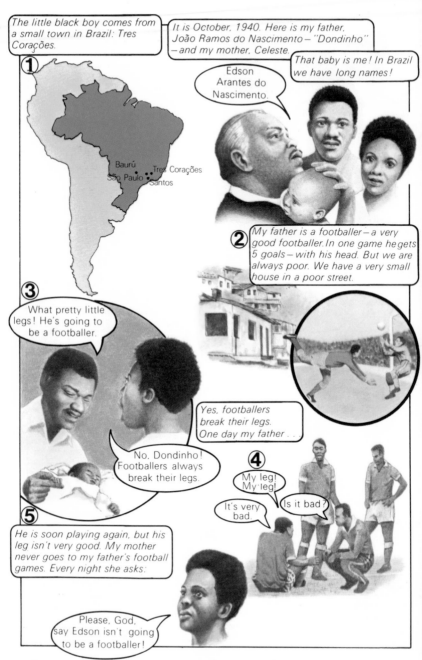

2

Every day I play football in our street with the boys.

1 Hey! Dico's good!

2 My father is happy.

O.K. But you have two feet, Edson.

That's good. Now do it again.

3 But my mother isn't happy.

You're not going to play football today, Edson. You're going to go to school.

No, Mama! I don't like my teacher. She's nasty.

4 Pelados is the name of the children's street-football.

Hey, Dico! Come and play pelados!

No, I'm going to school.

That's not my name!

Pelé! Pelé!

You're the king of the pelados — Pelé! Pelé!

I've got a new name now, but I don't like it!

Come here, Edson!

4

Yes, we are bad boys. It's a very sad story

1 We can't buy our shirts and shoes with this. Come on, Pelé, we're going to go to the peanut store again. You boys can come too.

2 Take the bag and give it to Pelé. Take it!

They're coming.

3 Now we're going to take them to the hills. Come with me.

Ten bags!

4 This is the place. We can put them in here. You're small, Benjamin, you can take them in.

Look at the sky — it's going to rain.

5 It's a very sad story . . .

I'm never going to go to that peanut store again!

6 Oh no! Benjamin is in there!

7

And the 7 September Club play in their socks.

8

1954. I'm in the Baurú Stadium again. B.A.C Junior are playing in the Avelone Junior Cup. We win the cup.

①

② Your boy plays beautiful football, Dondinho.

③ I'm going to go to São Paulo, Dondinho. Can Edson come with me? He can play in the Santos team. He can make a lot of money there.

EXIT

Thanks, Valdemar, but what is Celeste going to say?

④ Good morning, Celeste. I'm here again. What do you say? He can make a lot of money at Santos.

No, Valdemar. He's only a baby.

⑤ Good evening, Celeste. What do you say now?

What do you say, Celeste?

What do you say, Mama?

⑥ They're going to take my baby! "You're a man," they say. Go, Edson, go to Santos. Go and be a footballer!

⑦ I can't eat.

Have you got your food, Edson?

Bus Station

Goodbye, Mama! One day you're going to have a beautiful house. I'm going to buy it.

10

11

(1) *I want my mother and father. My game isn't very good.*

It's your ball, Pelé.

Lula's going to say "You can go to Baurú, to your father and mother. We don't want you."

(2) Pelé, you can go . . .

Yes, Mr Lula?

. . . and eat, Pelé, eat! Look at your thin little legs.

Yes, Mr Lula.

(3) *One morning . . .*

I'm always going to be small. They don't want me in Santos. Baurú can have me.

(4) Hello, Pelé. What are you doing?

Oh yes? Does Mr Lula know?

Oh hello, Big Sabu. I'm . . . er . . . going to Baurú.

No, he doesn't know. He's in bed.

Give your bag to me. Go and eat a big breakfast. We want you here, Pelé.

Sept 7, 1956. It's a big day. I am playing in the Santos team.

(5) Pelé! Pelé!

It's a goal! Telé—no, Pelé—puts it in.

And there's a new player on the field— the new Santos man Telé.

That's me in the number 10 shirt. Telé is the name of a footballer — but he never plays in the Santos team.

(6) That beautiful house is coming to you, Mama.

60,000 cruzeiros a year.

12

The new Brazilian team play the Corinthians in São Paulo.

①

② Corinthians! Corinthians! Who are these little boys? Go to your mothers!

We score three goals and they score only one. They play a very nasty game.

③ My knee! My knee!

Now I can't go to Stockholm.

④ It's bad, but you can go to Europe.

Is it very bad, doctor?

Can I play?

I don't know. I can't say.

⑤ We go to Italy. We win our games but my knee is bad and I don't play.

I'm not going to play in Sweden.

The doctor's going to look at your knee again today.

⑥ You can go to Sweden, but your knee isn't very good.

What do you say, doctor?

⑦ In Sweden, Brazil play two of their World Cup games, but . . .

June 14, 1958. Tomorrow Brazil are going to play Russia.

I'm never going to play again.

What do you say, doctor?

⑧ I'm going to say . . . he can play.

I can play!!!

We play Russia, Wales and France. Brazil win those three games. Now it's the big game. Brazil – Sweden.